# NEVER

## THE TOFFEES

## The Ultimate EVERTON

## QUIZ BOOK

### GAVIN BUCKLAND

The History Press

First published 2013

The History Press
The Mill, Brimscombe Port
Stroud, Gloucestershire, GL5 2QG
www.thehistorypress.co.uk

British Library Cataloguing in Publication Data.
A catalogue record for this book is available from the British Library.

ISBN 978 0 7509 5355 9

Typesetting and origination by The History Press
Printed in Great Britain

# Contents

# Introduction

**T**hat old chestnut about knowledge equalling power is never truer than when talking about football. Clubs around the country all have a number of followers who can recite, on request, the result of every game their team has played, the scorers and, for the really advanced, the date of the match. That is certainly the case with Everton.

These privileged and admired few are called into arbitrate disputes over the answers to questions such as who scored the fourth goal against Sheffield United in 1993, the identity of the bloke with the glasses who ran on the pitch at Anfield after Sharpie's goal, and the name of the dog who claimed an assist for West Brom against us at the Hawthorns in 1976 – unknown, but it was a terrier and if you don't believe the story, check the match report!

Thankfully, this book is not aimed at those lucky enough to know everything about the Toffees. It's aimed at all Evertonians, to be read especially on the way to the game – but not during, the exception being if bored when 4–0 up against Liverpool – either on the bus or in the car. Always welcome on away journeys, in my experience, are those who like asking football questions, but only if they bring some.

The format is pretty straightforward. There are forty rounds of questions on the mighty Blues, with eleven teasers per round.

In my experience the secret of a good quiz question is giving everybody an opportunity for a decent guess, and hopefully that is the case for most contained here. Most of the questions are on the modern era, so if your particularly expertise is the names and careers of our 1906 FA Cup final winning team, deepest apologies. Be warned though, there are a couple of stinkers.

This means the range of questions is as uncomplicated and straightforward as a Peter Reid pass: the Toffees in the Premier League, the FA Cup and League Cup and so on. Some regarding the David Moyes' era needed re-editing after the Scot, with no consideration to the production timetable of the book, decided to relocate down the M62.

Researching and compiling the questions was a hugely enjoyable experience, and I hope you have as much fun answering them!

*Gavin Buckland, 2013*

A quick note on the content: things can move quickly in the football world, so worth pointing out that the questions and answers are factually correct as at the start of the 2013/14 campaign, but that may change of course.

# Warming up

The quiz equivalent of the pre-match kick-in. Here are 11 questions that will hopefully act as a gentle introduction to the big game. Although some are a bit taxing, a few should be as easy as putting the ball in the net from a few yards out (though that, of course, has been beyond a few players over the years!).

1  Who did David Moyes succeed as Everton boss in March 2002?

2  How many separate spells in charge of Everton did Howard Kendall have?

3  Who has played the most games for the Toffees – 751 in total?

4 And who has scored the most goals for the club in the post-war era – 159 in all?

5 Who captained Everton when we won the FA Cup for the first time in thirty-three years, in 1966?

6 In which year were Everton last crowned League Champions?

7 What is the name of the church situated in the corner of Goodison Park, between the Main Stand and the Gwladys Street End?

8 In Joe Royle's first game in charge, against Liverpool in November 1994, which legendary striker became the first on-loan player to score for Everton in the Merseyside derby?

9 Who joined Everton from Tranmere Rovers in 1925 for a fee of £3,000?

10 Which English top-flight landmark was Everton the first to achieve in the 2002/03 campaign?

11 Which striker came to Everton from Leicester City for a club record fee of £850,000 in the summer of 1985?

# Twenty-First Century Toffees

After a difficult beginning, the Toffees have been Premier League stalwarts throughout the twenty-first century, and have regularly finished the league in the top ten. These questions test your knowledge of Everton during that time.

1   Which defender came to Everton from Celtic on a free transfer in the summer of 2001?

2   In the 2–1 victory over Arsenal in October 2002, Wayne Rooney famously scored his first Premier League goal and won the game, but who scored the earlier equaliser for the Toffees?

3   Who became the Toffees' third most expensive player at the time when moving to Goodison for a fee of £9 million in the summer of 2009?

4 In February 2000 who scored a hat-trick for Everton in the 4–0 away win at West Ham United?

5 James Vaughan became the youngest Premier League scorer at the age of 16 years 271 days when netting during a 4–0 win over which side in April 2005?

6 Which team did Everton beat for the first time in ten years with a 2–1 victory at Goodison in February 2010?

7 Who knocked Everton out of the League Cup twice in 3 seasons, in 2003/04 and 2005/06?

8 Which American international played 8 games on loan during the 2002/03 campaign, scoring 4 goals?

9 Against Newcastle at Goodison in December 2006 who became the second youngest Everton player to score two goals in a post-war league game, doing so aged 18 years 251 days?

10 Who captained Everton for the first and so far only occasion, in the 3–3 draw against Chelsea in December 2009?

11 In the 2006/07 campaign, who became the first Everton outfielder for twenty years to play every minute of a league season?

# Toffees Captains

One of the proudest achievements for any Everton player is being appointed club skipper. Indeed, less than fifty have held that honour since Nick Ross was the first to do so in the 1880s. This round looks at those lucky few who have worn the armband.

1 Who succeeded Kevin Ratcliffe as club skipper in January 1992?

2 Who was appointed captain during the summer of 2001?

3 Against Newcastle United in February 1998, who was the first overseas player to captain Everton in a first-team game?

4  Who skippered Everton for the first time in a 2–2 draw against Newcastle at Goodison in October 2008 – the only match Phil Neville missed during the season?

5  Who succeeded Howard Kendall as skipper after the future managerial legend left to join Birmingham in 1974?

6  Who captained the club for the first time against Luton in April 1984, and wore the armband for the last time against Wimbledon four years later?

7  Who was never appointed club captain but unusually skippered Everton, away at Spurs in the 1996/97, 1999/00, 2000/01 and 2002/03 seasons?

8  Who took over the captaincy of the side after Phil Neville was injured against Fulham in September 2009?

9  Who skippered Everton for the first time in the Merseyside derby match at Anfield in March 1981, before later losing the club captaincy for being overweight?

10  Who followed Brian Labone as skipper of the club in 1970?

11  Who scored in 2 of his first 3 Premier League matches as captain – against Stoke City in October 2009 and Manchester City in March 2013?

# Them and Us

Only a few players have been on the books of both clubs in Liverpool. A privileged few are held in the highest regard by both sets of supporters, while others have been known to get a bit of stick. Good or bad, red and blue, all the answers are those who have either bravely crossed the great divide direct or done so following a few stops on the way.

1  Who was the first player to be capped by England when playing for both teams?

2  Who scored his only Everton hat-trick against Coventry City in September 1991?

3  Who missed a penalty in his second Everton game at Southampton in March 1998?

4   Billy Hartill played for both teams during the 1935/36 season – who was the next player to appear for both teams during the same top-flight season?

5   Who left Everton for Sheffield Wednesday in a £275,000 deal in 1988?

6   In 2006, who was the most recent former Liverpool player to appear for Everton?

7   There have been two player/managers at both Merseyside clubs – Howard Kendall and Kenny Dalglish – but who was the only player to appear with both at each club when they were a player/manager?

8   In the 2000 Euros and the 2002 World Cup, who was the first player to appear in the final stages of an international tournament while playing with both sides?

9   In 1990, who was the first Everton player to take part in a penalty shoot-out at the World Cup finals?

10   In October 1982, who was the first Everton player to have a goal announced on the new Park End scoreboard at Goodison, having been the second player to do so on the original eleven years earlier?

11   Whose manager said it was like 'getting your right arm cut off' when he was sold to Everton in 1986?

# Round

## 5

# Transfer Trivia

During the 1960s, Everton were known as the 'Mersey millionaires', regularly buying players for big money. We have continued to spend in the transfer market, but in the modern era the Toffees have become one of the best clubs at polishing hidden diamonds bought at bargain prices. This round looks at the big moves, the loan deals and those whose Everton career did not go as planned.

1  In 2007, who was the first player brought to the club for a fee in excess of £10 million?

2  In 1994, who became the first player to move from Spurs to Everton?

3  In 1988, who left Everton to move to a Spanish club, six years after becoming the Toffees' record signing?

4  Which player was bought from French side RC Lens for a fee of £4.5 million in the summer of 2000?

5  In 1980, which future Premier League manager became the first player to join Everton on loan, later signing for us before joining Sheffield Wednesday twelve months later?

6 In 1991, who signed for Everton for a £1 million fee having previously been released as an 18 year old by the Toffees ten years before?

7 Two players from the starting line-up from the 1985 European Cup Winners Cup final later moved from Everton to which English side?

8 Which defender moved from Everton in 1977 to a Midlands' side, where he won League Championship and European Cup honours?

9 Who returned to Everton in the January 2006 transfer window, having left the previous summer?

10 Which forward was sold for a club record fee of £250,000 to Queens Park Rangers in March 1979, after less than twelve months at Goodison?

11 In 1994/95 who became the first of only 2 players to appear in the Premier League for 3 different clubs in the same season – moving from West Ham United to Everton and then to Coventry?

# Round 6

# We Love the 1970s

It was the era of Glam Rock, Punk and Disco. There was the three-day week, the long hot summer of 1976 and the winter of discontent. There were flares on the high street and flair on the football pitch. For the Toffees it was a mixed decade, as lady luck deserted us on a couple of memorable occasions. These questions test you on the decade that famously style forgot!

1  In which year was Everton great Alan Ball sold to Arsenal?

2  Which midfielder joined the Toffees for a club record fee of £500,000 from Nottingham Forest in August 1979?

3  Which Everton manager allegedly said, when drawn against Dukla Prague in the UEFA Cup, 'The second leg is not in Prague; it's in a place called Praha'?

4 The first replay of the 1977 League Cup final against Aston Villa is the last major domestic final not covered by TV, either live or by highlights – but on which ground was the 1–1 draw played?

5 Everton recorded the biggest top-flight victory of the decade by any team, when which side were on the receiving end of an 8–0 hiding at Goodison in November 1971?

6 Against which side did Bob Latchford famously score his thirtieth league goal of the season to claim a £10,000 newspaper prize in April 1978?

7 Now a common occurrence, why did Everton's home game in the FA Cup against West Brom in January 1974 make club history?

8 Who made the first of his 473 club appearances over eleven years at Nottingham Forest in March 1971, when his debut goal was not broadcast on BBC's *Match of the Day* as they cut to a newsflash just before it was shown?

9 Which future club captain was the Toffees' youngest player of the decade, making his debut against Manchester City in October 1976 aged just 18 years 6 days?

10 The Toffees made a return to European competition in 1975, but went out 1–0 on aggregate to which side in the UEFA Cup?

11 Who scored his 100th goal for the club against Ipswich Town in October 1971?

# Our Greatest Season Ever

No Everton quiz book worth the name would pass up the opportunity to have questions on our most successful ever campaign, that of 1984/85. Three trophies – yes, the Charity Shield does count – and an English record of forty-four victories in a single campaign has rightly made legends of both the manager and the squad. Relive some of the memories here.

1  How many of the other twenty-one teams in the top-flight did Everton beat in league matches?

2  Who scored our first goal of the campaign?

3  The Toffees played University College Dublin in the European Cup Winners Cup first round, but what was unusual about our kit for the second leg at Goodison?

4 Speaking of the Cup Winners' Cup, who scored for Everton in every round prior to the final?

5 Who scored the winning goal in the derby at Goodison in May 1985, having netted the winner for Grimsby Town against the Toffees on the same ground earlier in the campaign?

6 'Kevin Sheedy stood there directing operations like General Montgomery' – Peter Reid describing a mass brawl on which London ground just before Christmas 1984, and who was the Everton player sent off?

7 The Toffees collected the League Championship trophy on the night of a 3–0 home victory against which side in May 1985?

8 Who scored 4 league goals in the campaign – all scored away from home, in 3 games that brought the Toffees a vital 7 points?

9  Who performed a memorable finger-pointing exercise
   at an errant linesman in front of the *Match of the Day*
   cameras, after scoring the winner at Leicester in
   February 1985?

10  Who captained Everton for the first time in the 2–0
    defeat at Luton in the final game of the season?

11  Against which side did Kevin Sheedy famously score both
    times from a twice taken free-kick in a FA Cup quarter-
    final tie at Goodison?

# Overseas Blues

It's hard to believe that before the 1980s only one player born outside of the British Isles had appeared for the Toffees*, but since then our ranks have increasingly been filled with Blues from abroad. Some of them have rightly become modern-day legends while others have, for a variety of reasons, failed to make their mark. Here are a few testers on them:

1   In 1996, who was the first overseas player to score a hat-trick for Everton?

2   Juliano Rodrigo came to Goodison in 2002. He was the first player from which country to play for the club?

3   In 2002, which was the first country outside of the British Isles to field as many as 3 Everton players in a full international?

4  He was the only player from his country to score in the
first twenty years of the Premier League, and did so when
netting for Everton in the first week of the inaugural
season of 1992/93 – who is he?

5  Two players have appeared in the opening match of the
World Cup finals whilst at Everton – Ray Wilson in 1966,
and who else?

6  In 2003, who was the first overseas player to make 100
Premier League appearances for the Toffees?

7  Which overseas player remains the only Everton player
to score his only goal for the Toffees in a European game,
when doing so against Standard Liege at Goodison in
2008?

8  Italian Marco Materazzi was both bought from and sold
to which Italian club in the space of a year?

9   Which overseas player made just **6** appearances for the Toffees – one of which was in the FA Cup final?

10   Who made his Everton debut in the **2–2** draw at Southampton in February 2005?

11   Tim Cahill scored **68** goals for Everton – but which two clubs were his favourite opponents, the Aussie netting **7** against each?

\* The South African David Murray, who played briefly in the 1920s.

# The Swinging Sixties

The ten years of JFK, The Beatles and colour television was Everton's most consistently successful decade. Under the guidance of first Johnny Carey and then Harry Catterick we finished outside the top ten in the league only once as we re-established ourselves as one of the biggest clubs in the country, playing football in the real 'School of Science' tradition.

1   In which year did Harry Catterick join the club as manager, after John Moores infamously sacked Johnny Carey?

2   Which ground staged the 1966 FA Cup semi-final between Everton and Manchester United, when Colin Harvey's late goal took the Toffees on to Wembley?

3   Who scored a hat-trick for Everton in the final home game of three successive seasons from 1960/61 onwards?

4 Who scored 32 goals for the Toffees in 1964 – the most by an Everton player in a calendar year since the days of Dixie Dean?

5 Whose father famously had to repaint his red sports car blue after signing for Everton in 1967?

6 Who was sent off for the only time in his Everton career in a home game against Newcastle in March 1968?

7 Everton's biggest victory of the decade was 7–1 in November 1968, but over which side?

8 Lead by the legendary Jock Stein, which Scottish club were Everton's first-ever European opponents in the old Fairs Cup in 1962?

9 In January 1966, where did Joe Royle become Everton's then youngest ever player. Boss Harry Catterick was manhandled after the game by a group of fans who were angered at the dropping of Alan Young?

10 Which hugely significant figure in the club's history signed for the Toffees for a fee of £23,000 on the last day of 1965?

11 What famous programme was first broadcast on BBC1 on 7 April 1968?

# The 1980s and 1990s Finals

The Toffees were Wembley regulars across the two decades, reaching five FA Cup finals during that time, some ending in heartbreak and others memorably with tears of joy for the Toffee hordes who invaded the twin towers. Here's your starting XI with questions on the finals of 1984, 1985, 1986, 1989 and 1995.

1 In 1989, who became the first Everton player since Mike Trebilcock to score 2 goals in an FA Cup final?

2 Who were the three players to appear for Everton in all four finals during the 1980s?

3 Paul Rideout scored the winner in 1995, after which player's shot struck the bar?

4  In 1986, who became the first Everton player to appear as a substitute in an FA Cup final doing so against Liverpool?

5  Who was the only player to appear against the Toffees for two different teams in the five finals?

6  Who enlivened the 1984 final by donning a pair of Elton John glasses on the pitch after the game?

7  Who played his final game for the club in the 1989 final against Liverpool at Wembley, five years after making his debut against the same club on the same ground?

8  Who was the only Manchester United player to face us in the 1985 and 1995 finals?

9  Who replaced the injured Neville Southall in goal for the 1986 final?

10  Who was the only Everton outfield player who could not wear the specially designed shirt for the 1984 final against Watford, and why?

11  Which Manchester United player appeared against us in 1995, having also played against the Toffees on the way to the 1984 final?

# A Mixed Bag

We have just passed the halfway point in the first half, so we are breaking away from specialist rounds to one that is a real mixture of questions from over the years.

1   In 2013, who became the first Everton player to score in the FA Cup third round in four successive seasons?

2   Which was the first full season that Goodison was fully seated?

3   Who made 129 consecutive appearances for Everton from August 2006 to February 2009?

4   Who did Howard Kendall say this about in 1985: 'He was a big-time player who needed the big stage, which I was no longer able to provide him at Goodison, so he needed to move on.'

5 In 1976/77, who became the first Everton player to score in a League Cup and FA Cup semi-final in the same season?

6 What caused a suspension in play at Goodison for the only time ever, in a match against Manchester United in December 1975?

7 Which two teams played in the most recent full international staged at Goodison, in June 1995?

8 Who was the first Everton player to score 2 goals in our triumphant 1994/95 FA Cup winning campaign?

9 Who are the only two post-war players to be capped for England whilst playing for Everton, who happen to have the same surname?

10 In the 1998/99 season, who became the first Everton player to be sent off in all three domestic competitions in the same campaign?

11 Who, on New Year's Day 2012, became the first Everton player to appear in a century of Premier League victories for the Toffees?

# Penalty Prizes

It should be the easiest thing in football, scoring from 12 yards, but history says that is not necessarily the case, as you'll see here. Can you keep your nerve to provide the answer that's equivalent to sticking the ball into the bottom corner with the keeper diving the other way?

1  Which two players hold the Everton record for most successful penalties – netting 23 spot kicks apiece?

2 Duncan Ferguson scored his final goal for the club in May 2006, at the second attempt, after his spot kick was saved against which side?

3 Everton history was made against Bolton in February 2009, when, for the first time ever, two players scored from the spot for us in the same game – who were they, one of whom was making their debut?

4 Against Metalist Kharkiv in the UEFA Cup in 2007, who became the first Everton player to miss from the spot twice in the same home match?

5 Who is the only player to miss Premier League penalties, both playing for and against the Toffees?

6 In February 2009, which Aston Villa player became the first visiting player to score an FA Cup penalty at Goodison since Bill Shankly, for Preston, sixty-three years before?

7   Which 1960s legend missed just 1 of 20 spot kicks for the
    Toffees, at White Hart Lane in March 1962?

8   Which Everton legend fired wide from the spot against
    the Toffees when playing his final English top-flight match,
    for Southampton in 1982?

9   Who took only 2 penalties in his Everton career, one
    successfully in a 1968 FA Cup semi-final against Leeds,
    which took us to Wembley?

10  In the famous 3–2 victory over Wimbledon in 1994,
    Graham Stuart converted a first-half penalty after which
    Everton player fell theatrically (let's be honest!) in the
    area?

11  Who famously tried to take a spot kick while still wearing
    his tracksuit in the penalty shoot-out against Sunderland
    during a 1998 League Cup tie at Goodison?

# The Moyes Years

Now regarded as one of the best managers around, Moyes left the Toffees in the summer of 2013 with the goodwill of all Everton supporters, having transformed the fortunes of the club since he joined in 2002. His eleven years in charge represented the second longest single spell in charge for any Everton boss, and here are a few questions to test your knowledge of that time.

1   Which team did he face on the most occasions as manager – thirty-two times in total?

2   In 2003, who was the first Everton player to score a hat-trick for the Scot?

3   Who made his Everton debut against Wigan in 2007 and started his second spell against the same opponents in 2012?

4  In which season under Moyes did Everton record more league victories away from home than at Goodison (9 wins against 8)?

5  Against which side was the Scot unbeaten in his first 18 matches in charge, winning 13 and drawing 5?

6  Which future Everton player appeared against the Toffees in Moyes' first game in charge, against Fulham in March 2002?

7  During the 2009/10 season, against which side did Everton score 11 times in 3 matches, including a 5–1 win at Goodison and a 4–0 win away from home in the League Cup?

8  In the 2002/03 League Cup, against which team did the Toffees record their first penalty shoot-out victory in a cup tie for more than thirty years, after a 3–3 draw?

9  Who was the Toffees' leading scorer for the only time in the 2005/06 campaign, with 11 goals?

10  Wayne Rooney became the club's then youngest scorer when netting his first Everton goals in a 3–0 victory against which side in a League Cup match in October 2002?

11  Against which side did Everton record away wins in four successive seasons from 2007/08 to 2010/11?

# The League Cup

The competition that started more than fifty years ago has been a source of much frustration for the Blues in that time, with Everton still to lift the cup. Having said that, such were our priorities that we did not compete in the competition for most of the 1960s, and since then we have reached the final and have been semi-finalists on a number of occasions.

1   Who scored in a League Cup semi-final for the Toffees in 1988, on the same ground where he had previously netted in an FA Cup semi-final?

2   Who has made the most appearances for the Toffees in the competition – 65 in total?

3  In the 5–1 victory over Huddersfield in August 2010, who had the dubious distinction of being the first Everton player to miss a penalty and concede an own goal in the same game?

4  Who scored his first goals for Everton in a 5–0 win over Leyton Orient in this competition during August 2012?

5  Which side did Everton play in the semi-final for the first time under David Moyes?

6  Which future Toffees player scored against Everton for Aston Villa at Villa Park in their 1984 semi-final?

7  In the tie against Chelsea at Goodison in October 2011, what happened for the first time in an Everton game since a match against the same opponents twenty-six years before?

8 Who was the Everton keeper who saved a spot kick from Cardiff City's Billy Ronson in August 1979, later admitting it was because the same player had practised penalties against him for several years when they were at Blackpool?

9 Later credited with kick-starting the mid-1980s revolution under Howard Kendall, who were Everton's opponents in the third round in November 1983 that featured a last minute Graeme Sharp winner?

10 Who scored 2 goals in the same game for Everton for the only time in the 3–0 win at Sheffield Wednesday in September 2007?

11 Which Aston Villa player appeared against the Toffees in the 1977 final and eight years later was in the Manchester United side that faced Everton in the FA Cup final?

# A Mixed Bag of Toffees

This does what it says on the tin, a real potpourri of questions on the mighty Blues.

1 In 2012, who became the third oldest Everton player (in the post-war era) to appear for England in a full international?

2 Which former player had two spells as caretaker manager of the Toffees, after the departure of Colin Harvey in 1990 and Howard Kendall three years later?

3 Who twice scored at both ends against Watford for Everton – at Vicarage Road in September 1984 and at Goodison two years later?

4   Who once played in just 8 games of a season but was still the club's leading scorer for the campaign, with 9 goals?

5   Who was club captain before the appointment of Phil Neville in January 2007?

6   In October 2009, what coloured kit did Everton wear for the first and so far only time at Spurs in the League Cup?

7   Which player's injury lead to Paolo di Canio memorably stopping play when in a scoring position at Goodison in December 2000?

8   Which Lancashire club has had three managers (Johnny Carey, Gordon Lee and Howard Kendall) who have also taken charge of Everton?

9   Which country did Everton visit on a pre-season tour in 2010, only the third time the Toffees have played there?

10  Who played 389 games from 1963–1974, scoring 24 goals?

11  Harry Catterick, Howard Kendall and David Moyes have all taken charge of Everton in more than 500 games, but which manager is next highest on the list with 339 matches?

# Academy for Boys

Everton are acknowledged as having one of the most productive youth academies in English football, supplying a steady stream of graduates who have gone on to play for the Blues and have long and productive careers. Some of their achievements are documented here:

1 Who, when netting against Aston Villa in February 2009, became the youngest scorer in the FA Cup for Everton in the post-war era?

2   Leon Osman's first goals at Goodison came against which side in a 2–1 victory in August 2004?

3   Who became the club's youngest player when appearing against Blackburn at the age of 16 years 191 days, on the opening day of the 2008/09 campaign?

4   Who, when scoring against Fulham in January 2004, became the first on-loan player to score for Everton in the FA Cup?

5   Who was sent off for the only time in his Everton career at Birmingham City on Boxing Day 2002?

6   Who scored from our fourth penalty in the FA Cup semi-final penalty shoot-out against Manchester United at Wembley in 2009?

7  Who, in 1997, became Everton's second youngest goalscorer in a Merseyside derby after the legendary Tommy Lawton?

8  Who moved to Glasgow Rangers for a reported fee of £6 million in the summer of 2001?

9  Which Academy graduate failed to score in 72 Everton appearances between 1997 and 2000, but scored twice for his country in that time?

10  Who played 9 games for Everton before joining Grimsby in 2001, where he scored a famous cup winner at Anfield before becoming the League Two top-scorer with Yeovil in 2004/05?

11  Who won 8 caps for England Under-21s when at Everton before subsequently playing for Blackpool, Southend and Huddersfield after leaving Goodison in 2004?

# The Lee
# Years

Better known as a footballing firefighter, Gordon Lee joined Everton in 1976/77, when we were struggling in the league but were still in two cup competitions. He departed four years later, empty-handed, after an incident-packed time in charge when it was a case of so near and yet so far for his team. Will you be luckier in tackling these eleven questions?

1   Which club did Lee depart in January 1977 to become Everton manager?

2   An unbeaten 22-match run came to a crashing halt on Boxing Day 1977, with a 6–2 defeat to which side at Goodison?

3 The end of his reign neared following a defeat in the FA Cup sixth round to which side, following a replay in March 1981?

4 Which crowd favourite was sold to Chelsea for a fee of £165,000 in September 1978?

5 Everton went top of the table for the first time in four years, following a 4–1 defeat of Bristol City in February 1979. Who scored the only hat-trick of his Everton career in the game?

6 Which Everton player became only the second player to be sent off in an FA Cup semi-final in the 1980 clash against West Ham at Villa Park?

7 Which striker was leading scorer in the 1980/81 campaign with 19 goals in all competitions?

8   At the start of the 1979/80 season, the Toffees' shirts displayed sponsors logos for the first time – what was the name of the food company?

9   Which Everton legend was given his debut by Lee in the goal-less draw at Old Trafford in March 1980?

10   The Toffees beat which team 8–0 in a League Cup tie in August 1978, with Bob Latchford netting 5 goals?

11   In the 1978/79 season, Lee took the unusual step of announcing two captains: Mick Lyons was to be the skipper on the pitch, with which player taking the role the rest of the time?

# Premier League Toffees

Despite the odd alarm when the trapdoor to the league below threatened, the Toffees have been ever-presents in the Premier League since the inaugural season in 1992/93. It has been a case of a tale of two decades: during the first ten years we finished in the top six only once but since then, thanks to the shrewd management of David Moyes, we have engineered no less than nine finishes in the top eight.

1   Who, in 2004, became the first Everton player to make 300 Premier League appearances?

2   In the famous 1–1 draw against Coventry that secured Premier League survival in May 1998, who scored our goal and whose missed penalty shredded a few nerves?

3 In January 1994, Everton hit 6 goals for the first time in the Premier League during Mike Walker's first league game in charge, but against which side?

4 In the first twenty years of the Premier League, which side did the Toffees beat on the most occasions (sixteen times in all)?

5 In February 2006, against which side did the Toffees make history when two goalkeepers made their Premier League debut for one team in the same game?

6 Which goalkeeper kept 24 clean sheets in his 70 appearances – the second-best ratio for a Toffees' stopper in the Premier League, after Nigel Martyn?

7 In the spring of 1996, who became the first Everton player to net in 4 successive Premier League matches?

8  After Tony Hibbert, which outfield player has made the most Premier League appearances for Everton without scoring, this defender making 74 from 1995–1997?

9  Who scored our 1,000th Premier League goal when equalising against Spurs at Goodison in December 2012?

10  Which side had three different hat-trick scorers against Everton in their first three Premier League encounters in 1992/93 and 1993/94?

11  Who scored his first Premier League goal for the Toffees in his 205th Premier League appearance for Everton in January 2012?

# The Number Nines

The number nine shirt is the Toffees' most prized, having been worn by some of the greatest and well-loved players in the club's history, from Dixie Dean through to Dave Hickson, followed by the legends of the 1960s and 1970s in Alex Young and Bob Latchford respectively. Into the 1980s it was the turn of Graeme Sharp and Andy Gray. In tribute, here are eleven questions on some of our centre forwards.

1  Against which side did Louis Saha score four times in a Premier League game in February 2011?

2  Which striker was signed from St Johnstone in 1974 and sold to Newcastle United four years later?

3   Aiyegbeni Yakubu netted Everton's third European hat-trick against which side in the UEFA Cup at Goodison in February 2008?

4   Graeme Sharp scored 1 FA Cup semi-final goal for Everton – against which side?

5   Which striker scored on his Everton debut against Watford on the opening day of the 2006/07 campaign?

6   Bob Latchford scored at Goodison for which side on his first game back at the club in December 1981?

7   And which former Everton striker scored the final goal of his career in April 1981 for Norwich City – appropriately at Goodison Park?

8   Of which striker did Gordon Lee say: 'His speed may frighten our opponents but his finishing frightens me'?

9   And which striker did Brian Labone say 'was about ten stone wet through. He looked as athletic as Pinocchio.'

10  Dixie Dean's played and scored in one FA Cup final – a 3–0 victory over which side in 1933?

11  Nikica Jelavic's first goal for Everton was the only strike in a 1–0 victory over which side in March 2012?

# Round

# 20

# At the World Cup

A host of Blues have appeared in the World Cup finals, since full-back Alex Parker (of Scotland) became the first to do so in 1958. Some with differing degrees of success, from a World Cup winner to lasting just 60 seconds! (Note: unless stated otherwise, the players in question were at Everton at that time.)

1   Which Everton player scored his country's first ever goal at the World Cup finals, in Germany in 2006?

2   Who is the only Everton keeper to appear at the final stages of a World Cup?

3   Apart from players with England, who was the only Everton player to appear in the 1986 finals in Mexico?

4   Who has scored the most goals at the final stages whilst
    an Everton player?

5   Who was the only Everton player to appear in the 1994
    finals in the USA?

6   England's first ever substitute in the World Cup,
    in Mexico 1970, was an Everton full-back, who replaced
    another Toffees full-back in the group game against
    Romania. Can you name the two players involved?

7   Which Everton player's World Cup career at the final
    stages lasted only one minute, when coming on as a
    substitute for the Republic of Ireland against Saudi Arabia
    in 2002?

8   At the 2010 finals, who became the first Everton player to
    score a penalty in the final stages (excluding shoot-outs)?

9   Two players have appeared in the World Cup final when
    with the Toffees – Ray Wilson in 1966 and who else?

10  Who is the only player to score in a World Cup final,
    having played for Everton during his career?

11  Who is the only Everton player to score for Scotland in
    the final stages?

# The Harvey Years

Colin Harvey remains one of the club's greatest servants. Having started as a supporter as a child and ending as an influential member of our Youth Academy, over a period of forty years he also served Everton as a player, first-team coach and boss, after stepping up to become manager when Howard Kendall left in 1987. Here are some teasers on the three years that followed.

1  Harvey's first game in charge was a 1–0 victory in the Charity Shield over which team at Wembley?

2  For which Dutchman did the Everton boss pay £250,000 in the summer of 1989?

3  What club record, that still stands, did the Toffees set in Harvey's first season as boss, during 1987/88?

4   In the same season, which side did Everton play on no less than five occasions in January?

5   Which new striker's 6 goals in 7 games at the start of the 1989/90 campaign earned him an England call-up?

6   In the summer of 1988 the Toffees paid a transfer fee of £925,000 for the services of which player?

7   Who scored 13 goals in 35 appearances in his only full season for the club in 1989/90?

8   Whose goal brought a derby victory at Goodison in March 1988, as well as ending Liverpool's 29 unbeaten league game run from the start of the campaign?

9   Whose only goal at Goodison, in 236 appearances at the venue, was actually into his own net during the 3–2 victory over Charlton in April 1989?

10  In February 1989, which opposition player was sent off at Goodison for the second successive season?

11  Tony Cottee scored a hat-trick on his Everton debut against which side in August 1988, opening the scoring after just 34 seconds?

# The Magic of the FA Cup

It remains arguably the greatest and most romantic of all cup competitions, and the Toffees have enjoyed a glorious history, winning the FA Cup five times as well as reaching eight other finals, since our first appearance against Wolves in 1893. With more than 400 FA Cup games to choose from there was plenty of choice for these questions.

1  Who scored the winning penalty in the shoot-out victory over Manchester United in our 2009 semi-final?

2   The Toffees have played once at Anfield in the FA Cup in the last 100 years – who scored our goal in a 1–1 draw in the game in question?

3   The last team to lose to Everton in the competition in successive seasons were beaten 2–1 in the 1985 semi-final and 1–0 in the sixth round a year later – who are they?

4   Who was famously described by Joe Royle as the 'best substitute I never made' in 1995?

5   During the 1980s, who kept goal both for and against Everton in the semi-finals?

6   In the 2008/09 FA Cup campaign, which ended in a final defeat to Chelsea, who was the only Everton player to net more than once?

7   In January 2012, who were our first non-league opponents in the competition for more than twenty years?

8   Who were the only side we defeated in the competition in each of the last four complete decades, winning ties in 1971, 1988, 1990 and 2009?

9   Who is our leading post-war scorer in the FA Cup, with 20 goals in 54 games?

10  Who was rewarded for a famous FA Cup derby goal against Liverpool in January 1981 with a pie in the face from a spectator?

11  End with a difficult one – who was our unused substitute in the 1968 FA Cup final against West Brom?

# Quick off the Mark

Although we all love a last-minute winner (and hate ones against us as well) there's nothing like a goal straight from the kick-off to freshen the senses. There have been plenty over the years involving the Blues, although none faster than David Johnson's remarkable 6-second goal in the FA Youth Cup against Manchester United in 1969! Let's see if you're equally quick-thinking with these.

1 Who was the Fulham goalkeeper beaten by David Unsworth's 32-second strike in David Moyes' first game in charge, in March 2002?

2 In 2012, whose 49-second strike was the fastest by an Everton player at Goodison in the FA Cup for forty years, against Blackpool in the fifth round?

3  Who netted after just 45 seconds when Everton clinched
   the league title at Norwich in May 1987?

4  Who scored for the Toffees after just 48 seconds against
   Portsmouth at Goodison in March 2008?

5  Who scored after just 14 seconds against Chelsea in
   a 5–2 victory in March 1970 – the quickest goal by an
   Everton player at Goodison?

6  Whose 41-second strike for Everton at Anfield on Easter
   Saturday, April 1999, was our quickest goal on the ground
   for more than sixty years?

7  And two weeks later, who scored after just 42 seconds
   for us at St James Park, the first of 6 goals he scored for
   Everton on the ground?

8  Which Blackburn player netted after just 13 seconds at
   Goodison on Easter Saturday 1995, then the fastest-ever
   goal scored in the Premier League?

9  Which midfielder's strike, after just 23 seconds at
   Selhurst Park on New Year's Day 1996, remains our
   fastest Premier League goal?

10 After how many seconds did Louis Saha open the scoring
   against Chelsea in 2009, to record the fastest goal in
   FA Cup final history?

11 In the famous European Cup encounter against Borussia
   Mönchengladbach in November 1970, whose goal after
   just 23 seconds at Goodison remains our fastest scored
   in European competition?

# Toffees
# in Europe

Everton first played in European competition in 1962, and our history against teams on the continent is littered with ups and downs, from penalty shoot-out victories and defeats to the odd refereeing howler. We still have one European trophy in the cabinet though, from that unforgettable night in Rotterdam. These questions remind us of our travels abroad.

1   In 2009, who was the first Everton player to make 20 appearances for the Toffees in Europe?

2   Who created goals for both Andy Gray and Kevin Sheedy in the 1985 European Cup Winners Cup final?

3   In the famous semi-final against Bayern Munich in 1985, who scored our third goal?

4   Which Irish team did Everton record a club record two-leg aggregate victory of 10–0 in the 1978/79 UEFA Cup?

5   Who, when playing for Larissa at Goodison in the UEFA Cup in 2007, became the first former Everton player to play against the Toffees in Europe?

6   Who scored our first hat-trick in Europe, in a 6–2 home win over Keflavik in the European Cup in September 1970?

7   Which Dutch side are the only team to knock us out of Europe on two occasions, doing so in 1979/80 and 1995/96?

8   In the 2009/10 season, whose first 2 goals for Everton were in Europe, before he had even scored in a domestic match?

9   Which defender achieved the unusual distinction of being the only player to appear for the Toffees in the old Fairs Cup (1965/66) and its replacement, the UEFA Cup (1975/76)?

10  At Alkmaar, in December 2007, who became our youngest player to appear in Europe, aged just 16 years 284 days?

11  And which midfielder captained Everton for the second and final time in that game?

# Celtic Toffees

Right back to our early days in the nineteenth century, some of the greatest players to wear the Everton shirt have come from across the Irish Sea or the Welsh border. Thanks to the qualification rules, some of those who have played for those countries whilst a Blue may have been born elsewhere of course; either way, here's a few testers.

1   Which Everton player won his first international cap for the Republic of Ireland against Wales in February 2011?

2   Who was the Welsh international, signed by David Moyes during the summer of 2005 for a £3.5 million fee, who scored just 1 Premier League goal at Birmingham City before leaving eighteen months later?

3 Who was the Irish international signed from Chelsea for a £850,000 fee in December 1996?

4 Which Welshman scored the first goal of David Moyes' first full season in charge in 2002/03 before leaving for Fulham twelve months later?

5 Which Irish international was sent off on his final appearance for the Toffees at White Hart Lane in August 2006?

6 Which Welsh international scored Everton's first-ever Premier League goal?

7 Which two Irish internationals at Everton during the 1970s and 1980s shared the same name?

8 Who was the last Welshman to score a hat-trick for Everton?

9 Which Everton player was banned by FIFA from playing international football, after winning his first cap for the Republic of Ireland in 1981, before being reinstated two years later?

10 Which Welshman was part of Howard Kendall's 'Magnificent Seven' signings when he first became manager in 1981, but left later that year?

11 Which Everton player was born in Wales but played international football for the Republic of Ireland?

# The Championship Years

Everton have won the title on nine occasions, the first being in the third season of league football in 1890/91. Curiously, we were also title winners in gaps of twenty-four years afterwards: 1914/15, 1938/39, 1962/63 and 1986/87! Unfortunately the unlikely sequence stopped when we finished seventh in 2010/11. Thankfully most of the questions are on our post-war triumphs.

1  The Toffees clinched the title in 1984/85 after defeating which team 2–0 at Goodison on May Day?

2  Who was the top scorer in our 1969/70 league campaign with 23 goals?

3  Who kept goal for the Toffees in their 1962/63 and 1969/70 title-winning seasons?

4   Who, in the 1986/87 season, became the only Everton player in the post-war era to win a championship medal in his only season at the club?

5   Against which title rivals did Everton clinch a famous 2–1 victory in April 1985, in a match made famous by a remarkable late save by Neville Southall?

6   Only one player scored a hat-trick for Everton in the 1986/87 League season, who did so in the 3–0 home win over Newcastle on Easter Monday?

7   We set a club record in 1969/70 for the fewest defeats in a league campaign – how many did we suffer?

8   Who was the Sheffield Wednesday player signed for a record fee of £55,000 in December 1962, subsequently playing a key role in the title triumph?

9   Who was the only player to start all 42 league games of the 1986/87 season?

10  Who was the legendary striker who was top scorer (with 34 league goals) for the Toffees in the 1938/39 Championship season?

11  Two outfielders won title-winners' medals in 1962/63 and 1969/70 – Brian Labone and who else?

# The
# Derby

Having first locked horns as far back as 1894, the Merseyside derby remains the most highly charged and passionate contest in English football, with Everton and Liverpool facing each other more than 200 times in all competitions – more than any other domestic fixture. With all of that history there is plenty of stuff to test you on – do you play it tight or go for the jugular?

1　Who scored 5 league goals for Everton in post-war derby matches, the most for the Toffees in that time?

2　Which Everton player has played in the most derby matches – 41 in total?

3　Who is the only player to score for Everton from the spot more than once in derby games?

4　Whose only derby goal for Everton came for the Toffees in the 2–0 victory at Goodison in October 2010?

5　Which Everton boss famously never lost a derby game?

6　Who holds the Everton record for playing in the most derby matches (18 matches) before netting his first goal against Liverpool?

7   Who came on as a substitute for Everton in the 1984
    League Cup final replay against Liverpool, becoming the
    only player to appear for the club in both the 1977 and
    1984 finals?

8   At Anfield in October 1979, who became the first
    Everton player sent off in the fixture for eighty-
    three years, in a clash that also saw Liverpool's Terry
    McDermott dismissed?

9   In the September 1999 clash at Anfield, which surname
    was common to a player from each side, and was the last
    time this happened?

10  Who scored our goal in the 1–1 drawn Charity Shield
    game at Wembley in August 1986?

11  The closest two brothers have come to facing each other
    in the derby was in March 1988. Who started the game
    for Everton while his brother stayed on the substitutes'
    bench for the Reds?

# Round
## 28

# The Toffees and Manchester

Just 30 miles down the road, the city of Manchester has historically been one of our closest rivals in more ways than one. Given the geographical proximity, Everton have shared a fair number of players (and managers) with both Manchester City and United, as well as facing the two clubs in a number of significant games over the years, from crucial league matches to Wembley FA Cup finals – plenty to look at here then.

1  In 2012, who became the first Everton player to score league goals at both Manchester clubs in the same calendar year?

2  And on a similar theme, in the inaugural Premier League season of 1992/93, who was the last Everton player to score league goals at both United and City in the same campaign?

3  In our famous 1–0 win over Manchester United at Goodison in April 2005, who became the first United player ever to be sent off on the ground?

4  Which two Everton substitutes scored against United in a 3–1 victory at Goodison in February 2010?

5  Which former Everton keeper joined City in the summer of 2012?

6  Who scored his first Everton goal from open play at the City of Manchester Stadium during a 2–1 win for the Toffees in December 2010?

7  Who scored for Everton in a Merseyside derby in September 1990, a year after netting for City in a Manchester derby?

8  League history was made at Maine Road in April 1993, when how many goalkeepers played in a 5–2 away win for the Toffees?

9  Which former Everton defender played for Manchester City in the 2007/08 season?

10  In a 3–3 draw with United in April 1982 at Goodison, which defender played in goal as a replacement for the injured Neville Southall – the last outfielder to don the keeper's gloves for Everton in a game on the ground?

11  Which former Everton skipper played for Manchester United in the 1985/86 campaign?

# Who Am I?

More than 800 players have appeared for Everton's first team in the past 125 years or so, so plenty to choose from in a 'Who am I?' round. Some, of course, have enjoyed hugely successful careers, being celebrated as Everton greats. Others in comparison have barely registered a ripple of recognition, enjoying only minutes in the jersey.

1 Signed from Ipswich in 2004, the Toffees were one of his fifteen league clubs, and he scored some vital goals in the campaign that followed.

2 A Mancunian born in 1971, this player started his career as an apprentice at Wigan before becoming a key part of the 'Dogs of War' era under Joe Royle in the mid-1990s.

3  The Scandinavian who started in English football across
   the Pennines, after moving to Goodison he scored against
   England at the World Cup finals.

4  Classy defender who joined the club in the Walter
   Smith era and technically had two spells at the Toffees,
   the second lasting just one game.

5  One of our 1960s giants, this player joined Everton from
   a club in a capital city in another country, becoming a
   Goodison idol in seven years at the club.

6  An international player that was born in the
   northernmost town in England. One of the most
   talented players to appear for Everton, won League
   titles in three different countries, including two whilst
   a Toffee.

7  Joined the Toffees for a fee of £750,000 in 1989, played
   for three years without scoring a goal but managed to net
   one for England during that time.

8   Classy midfielder signed by Billy Bingham during the 1970s from a Lancashire club, returning there after a five-year stay at Goodison.

9   Welshman who joined the club from Swansea and later broke the record for the most international caps for a goalkeeper from his country.

10  Can count Newcastle amongst his former clubs and played for their close rivals after leaving Goodison. He scored 35 goals in 115 appearances as an Everton player.

11  Nicknamed 'Diamond', this player scored 2 important goals on a crucial afternoon.

# Round
# 30

# Scottish Toffees

Back in the nineteenth century the vast majority of Everton players came from north of the border. Since then, Scottish players – and the odd manager – have wielded a huge influence on the club's fortunes, from steely defenders to midfield maestros and the odd prolific striker. Nobody can deny the influence of Scottish players on our fortunes.

1 From which Scottish side did Everton sign both Gary Naysmith and David Weir?

2 Which player, when with Everton, scored the winning goals for Scotland against both England and Germany in full internationals, the first player to achieve that feat for any country?

3 From which Scottish side did Everton sign Graeme Sharp for a fee of £120,000 in 1980?

4 Which Scot in the early 1990s became the first player to win international caps during their career at both Everton and Tranmere Rovers?

5 Two Scots made substitute appearances for us in the 1989 FA Cup final against Liverpool – Stuart McCall and who else?

6   Which Glaswegian winger won 1 cap for his country
    while signed with Everton, before moving on to
    Birmingham in 1976?

7   Which Scottish player made his Everton debut in the
    Merseyside derby at Anfield in April 1999?

8   Who is Everton's leading scorer for Scotland in full
    internationals, with 13 goals in total?

9   Which Scot featured in both Walter Smith's and David
    Moyes' first games in charge of Everton? He made his
    Everton debut in 1998 and then played for Fulham four
    years later.

10  Everton signed Stuart McCall from which club in the
    summer of 1988?

11  Which follically challenged full-back made 72
    appearances for the club after signing from Falkirk
    in 1971?

# Goals, Goals, Goals

We all love goals, from 30-yard screamers to tap-ins on the goal line. The Toffees have employed some of the most prolific strikers in the game over the years – including Dixie Dean, the greatest of them all – and also players elsewhere who knew where the old onion bag was. Easy round, this … only more than 8,000 goals to choose from.

1   Before Louis Saha in the 2009 FA Cup final, who had been the last Everton player to score at Wembley?

2   When we beat Metalist Kharkiv in the first round of the 2007/08 UEFA Cup, who scored in both legs for the Toffees?

3   Who scored on his Everton debut in a 2–1 victory at Bolton in September 2007?

4 Which English international scored just 10 goals in nearly 700 career league games, one of which was on his Goodison debut for Everton against Spurs in February 1993?

5 Who scored his first Everton goal against one of his former clubs, Aston Villa, at Goodison in December 1983?

6 After Dixie Dean, who has been Everton's only goalscorer in a game on most occasions – doing so 29 times?

7 Who scored one European goal for the Toffees, in the 2–0 win at Fortuna Sittard in the European Cup Winners Cup in March 1985?

8 Regarded as being a slightly temperamental overseas player, who scored on his Everton debut at Crystal Palace in January 1998?

9 Who was the first Everton player to score a goal in a League match televised live in this country – a 1–0 win at Chelsea in August 1984?

10 In September 1991, who was the last Everton player to score in 6 successive matches?

11 Between 1971 and 1978, who was the only Everton player to score in a league derby match, doing so at Anfield in October 1976?

# Round
# 32

# Between
# the Sticks

They say you have to be a bit mad to be a keeper – can't possibly comment on that of course … Having said that there have been a number of Everton keepers who were regarded as being a bit eccentric, by team mates and supporters alike. What is beyond doubt is that more than a few were very good, with one laying claim to be one of the greatest of all time – wonder if he pops up here?

1 Which keeper made his Everton debut as a substitute for Neville Southall in the 7–1 victory over Southampton at Goodison in November 1996?

2 Who was the first Everton keeper to take part in a penalty shoot-out, against Borussia Mönchengladbach in the European Cup in 1970?

3 Who made 2 league appearances for Everton as a replacement for the injured Tim Howard in September 2007?

4 Which post-war goalkeeper has won a league title with Everton and another side?

5 Who played in goal for Everton in all 5 league games Neville Southall missed in the nine years after October 1987?

6 Whose only season at Goodison was the 1980/81 campaign, when he made 48 appearances?

7 From which club did Harry Catterick buy David Lawson for a record fee of £80,000 in the summer of 1972?

8 Steve Simonsen left Goodison in 2004 and joined which side on a free transfer?

9 Who made his only Everton appearance in the 4–3 defeat at Spurs in January 2003?

10 Which goalkeeper famously injured himself at Stamford Bridge before an FA Cup fourth round replay in February 2006, when he was warming up in a prohibited area?

11 Howard Kendall signed two keepers in the summer of 1981 – Neville Southall and who else?

# Golden Oldies

They are the ones we all secretly admire, those players old enough to play in the veterans' league on a Sunday morning but instead were turning up for the Blues on a Saturday afternoon (live television commitments permitting of course). The players who are the answers in this round are, on average, 35 years of age, but we start with someone even older.

1  Which legendary keeper is our oldest ever player, appearing in 1952 at the ripe old age of 42 years 282 days?

2  Who in April 2001 set a new record for being the club's oldest Premier League outfield player, at 39 years 23 days?

3  In the Europa League clash against BATE Borisov in December 2009, who made his only appearance for the Toffees aged 36 years 95 days?

4 Which outfielder made his final appearance for the Toffees aged 36 years 213 days, against Portsmouth in December 2006?

5 Who in 2012/13 became our oldest scorer in a League Cup game, aged 34 years 284 days?

6 Who was Everton's oldest player of the 1980s, appearing against West Ham in the FA Cup in January 1982, aged 35 years 225 days?

7 Likewise, who was our oldest player of the 1970s, appearing in his last game aged 32 years 3 days in the 1971 FA Cup semi-final against Liverpool?

8 Who scored his final goal for Everton at White Hart Lane against Spurs in August 2007, aged 35 years 312 days?

9 Who is Everton's third oldest hat-trick scorer, and oldest in the league since 1948, aged 32 years 181 days?

10 Who is the most recent player to appear for the club across three different decades?

11 Which 35-year-old was signed by Walter Smith in February 2002?

# One Last
# Mixed Bag

After a long break, here is the last bag of Toffees' treats, enjoy them while they last!

1  Who were Everton's last ever opponents in an FA Cup second replay?

2  Five Everton players, all with the same surname, each played in a different decade from 1960s onwards – what was the surname?

3  Which player from our 1985 European Cup Winners Cup final side was bought from, and sold to, the same club?

4  Including loan spells, who is technically the only player signed by Everton on four different occasions?

5 Who was the last Everton player to score a hat-trick when captaining the side?

6 In our best Premier League season in 2004/05, who scored the first and last goals of the campaign?

7 Who was the last father and son combination to play for Everton, in the 1970s and 1990s respectively?

8 Darron Gibson scored his first Everton goal against which side?

9 Which player, when at Everton, has made the most international appearances for a country outside of the British Isles?

10 Which player, in his 6 full seasons at Everton, was leading scorer in the league on five occasions?

11 Who appeared in the 2008 Olympic football final when with Everton (his country lost to Argentina in the game)?

# Premier League Teasers

Our second round of Premier League questions. In keeping with the major changes that have been brought in since 1992, feel free to answer the questions on a Sunday afternoon or a Monday evening.

1   Which overseas player was signed in the summer of 1994 and scored his first Everton goal in a 2–2 draw against QPR in September of that year?

2   Which two players have scored a record 16 Premier League goals against Everton?

3   On which ground did Everton record a first league win since 1951, thanks to a famous Wayne Rooney winner in November 2002?

4 Who was the first player to appear for Everton in 10 successive Premier League seasons?

5 And who was the first player to score for Everton in 10 successive Premier League seasons?

6 Which overseas outfielder has made the most Premier League appearances for the Toffees – 220 in total?

7 In the 2003/04 and 2011/12 campaigns, surprisingly the biggest league attendance at Goodison was not for the derby or Manchester United, but against another side – which one?

8 Everton's record Premier League defeat is 7–0, but to which side?

9 In the famous 4–4 draw with Manchester United in April 2012, who scored 2 of our goals?

10 At the end of the 2012/13 campaign, who has made a club record of 77 substitute appearances in the Premier League?

11 Tim Cahill's first home and away goals in the Premier League came against the same side – which one?

# What's the Link?

Rather than six degrees of separation, here there is only one. In each of the following there are three Toffees players, games or opponents. Your task is to find the missing link between the trios in the question. Some may be obvious, some perhaps not.

1   The 1980s utility man Alan Harper, the talismanic Duncan Ferguson and Steven Naismith?

2   The 1970s stars Bruce Rioch and Colin Todd, plus Joe Royle and stalwart Craig Short?

3   Steve Watson (Bristol City, 2004), Tim Cahill (Manchester United, 2009) and Leighton Baines (Chelsea, 2011)?

4   Birmingham City, Manchester City and Southampton in
    the 1985/86 campaign?

5   Newcastle United (1997/98), Blackburn Rovers
    (2006/07) and Oldham Athletic (2007/08)?

6   Graeme Sharp, Gary Stevens and Kevin Campbell?

7   Welsh 'man of steel' Barry Horne, the late Gary Speed
    and record-signing Andy Johnson?

8   Birmingham City (3–1, 1981), Norwich City (1–0, 1987)
    and Swindon Town (6–2, 1994)?

9   Legendary player and manager Joe Royle, steady full-back
    Neil Pointon and Academy graduate Jack Rodwell?

10  Joker John Bailey in 1981, Danish midfielder Claus
    Thomsen in 1997 and Phil Neville nine years later?

11  Manchester City, Nottingham Forest and Crystal Palace?

# Toffees Opponents

During 2012, the Toffees celebrated the 125th anniversary of their first-ever fixture, against Bolton Wanderers in the FA Cup. Since 1887 we have played in excess of 5,000 first-team matches against more than 130 different sides. For every Liverpool and Manchester United there is a Jarrow and Rapid Vienna (one game apiece, with one a little bit more memorable than the other), as you may find here.

1   Which side have Everton beaten more times than any other – 78 victories in 175 matches?

2   The most played fixture, though, in English league football history is between Everton and which other team, whom we have played 196 times?

3 Which side have we played four times in the Premier
  League, winning all 4 matches – 4–2 and 3–1 in 1999/2000
  and 2–1 and 3–0 in 2006/07?

4 Which club have beaten Everton on the most occasions –
  ninety-eight times at the end of the 2012/13 campaign?

5 We have played which team on nineteen occasions in the
  FA Cup, including twice in the final itself?

6 Which team have we faced only twice in the league,
  famously in 1974/75 when their two wins effectively cost
  Everton the title?

7 Which is the only English team we have faced in Europe?

8 And which side have we faced on most occasions
  in the League Cup – 11 times, most recently in
  November 2006?

9   Which club held the record for the most home games in European competition without ever losing – thirty-two in total, a sequence ended by a 3–2 win by Everton in the UEFA Cup in December 2007?

10  Against which side have we had the longest gap between fixtures in the Premier League – fifteen years from April 1996 to September 2011?

11  Which club had its 100 per cent record against Everton in the FA Cup (four wins in four ties) ended by a 2–1 win for the Toffees in the fourth round in January 2012?

# The HK File

Everton's Manager of the Millennium once likened being in charge of the club as being like a marriage. After starring as a player for the Blues in the 1960s and 1970s, he later became our most successful manager ever. Not a bad CV that!

1 From which club did we sign Howard in March 1967, for an £80,000 fee?

2 Howard's first Everton goal came against the team he had played against in the 1964 FA Cup final when aged just 17 – which side?

3 Which club was Howard managing before he returned to Goodison as boss in 1997?

4   Which former player was his assistant in his final season at Goodison?

5   In which year did he become Everton's club captain?

6   His last victory as Everton manager at Wembley was against which side?

7   Who did Kendall pick as his first Everton captain, for the 1981/82 season?

8   How many FA Cup finals did he feature in for Everton as player and manager?

9   Who was the Everton goalkeeper in his final game as manager against Coventry in May 1998?

10  In which year did he score a derby match winner against Liverpool at Goodison Park?

11  And finally, which famous and iconic singer, who rose to fame in the early 1970s, was in the same school team as him as a teenager?

# Round 39

# **More Derby Madness**

Watching the Merseyside derby can be sheer torture at times, so with that in mind here is another round of questions about the matches against our closest rivals.

1   Which two Everton players in the post-war era have played in three derby matches and scored 3 goals in total?

2   Which was the last neutral league ground to stage a derby match?

3   Who made his Everton debut against Liverpool at Goodison in October 1998, and missed an opportunity to score in the opening seconds?

4   In January 2011, who scored his first Premier League goal for the Toffees at Anfield?

5  Who was famously Everton's mascot in the Anfield derby of November 1996?

6  At the end of the 1977/78 season, which player had been responsible for both Everton and Liverpool's most recent derby victories at that time?

7  In which year was the famous FA Cup fifth round clash between the two teams that was watched by a combined crowd of almost 105,000, live at Goodison and on CCTV at Anfield?

8  Who replaced the injured Kevin Sheedy in the starting line-up for the 1984 League Cup final replay between the two sides?

9  Who is the only man to take temporary managerial charge of Everton for a derby game?

10  Who was the only Everton player to appear in both our 1981 and 1991 FA Cup victories against Liverpool?

11  Who scored his final 2 goals for Everton in an FA Cup tie against Liverpool?

# Injury Time
# Toffees

Right, after the quiz equivalent of 90 minutes of sheer torture, the fourth official says there are eleven added questions. Conveniently they are all on late drama involving the Toffees, all in the recent past. Hope you've enjoyed the quiz – 'C'mon you Blues!'

1  The record for the latest goal scored in an Everton game was after 97 minutes of play against Wigan at Goodison in September 2011. Which overseas player scored the goal, his first strike for the club?

2  At the end of the 2012/13 campaign, who was the last Everton player to score an extra-time Fa Cup winner in a match at Goodison?

3   In February 2013, Marouane Fellaini became the first
    Everton player in nineteen years to score 2 second-half
    league goals at the Park End at Goodison, including a 93rd
    minute equaliser – who were our opponents?

4   Who scored his first goal at Goodison in the 2–1 win
    over Wigan in August 2009, courtesy of an injury
    time penalty?

5   And who scored his first Premier League goal for the
    Toffees in the following campaign with an injury time
    equaliser – this time in a 1–1 draw against Bolton?

6   The first time that Everton scored 2 goals in added time
    was in a 3–1 Premier League victory at Goodison in
    November 2007, but over which side?

7   Which Everton player scored the final goal of the Premier
    League season in 2009/10, in the 92nd minute of the 1–0
    home win over Portsmouth?

8 Tim Cahill's first match as an orthodox centre forward for the Toffees in December 2008 saw the Australian head a last-minute winner against which side?

9 Manchester United were the victims of a double injury time strike by the Toffees in September 2010, but who scored our equaliser in the 3–3 draw?

10 Against which team did James McFadden score a spectacular last-minute volleyed winner at Goodison in April 2007?

11 One of the highlights of the 2004/05 campaign was a late, late home victory against Portsmouth, but who scored the winner in added time?

THE ANSWERS

# Warming up

1 Walter Smith.
2 Three – 1981–87, 1990–93 and 1997/98.
3 Neville Southall.
4 Graeme Sharp.
5 Brian Labone.
6 1987.
7 St Luke's Church.
8 Duncan Ferguson, who was on loan from Rangers and signed permanently later in the season.
9 Dixie Dean.
10 The first club to play 100 seasons in the English top-flight.
11 Gary Lineker.

1 Alan Stubbs.
2 Tomasz Radzinski.
3 Diniyar Bilyaletdinov.
4 Nick Barmby.
5 Crystal Palace.
6 Chelsea.
7 Middlesbrough.
8 Brian McBride, scoring 4 goals in 8 games.
9 Victor Anichebe – only Joe Royle (in 1967) was younger.
10 Tim Howard.
11 Joseph Yobo.

# Toffees Captains

1 Dave Watson.
2 Kevin Campbell.
3 Slaven Bilić.
4 Mikel Arteta.
5 Roger Kenyon.
6 Peter Reid.
7 David Unsworth.
8 Tim Cahill.
9 Billy Wright.
10 Alan Ball.
11 Leon Osman.

# Them and Us

1 Nick Barmby.
2 Peter Beardsley.
3 Don Hutchison.
4 Gary Ablett – the late defender doing so in 1991/92.
5 Alan Harper.
6 Sander Westerveld, who played 3 matches in February and March 2006 as emergency goalkeeping cover.
7 Steve McMahon (Everton 1981–83 and Liverpool 1985–91).
8 Abel Xavier (playing for Everton in 2000 and Liverpool two years later).
9 Kevin Sheedy (scored for Republic of Ireland against Romania).
10 David Johnson, who left Everton in 1972 for Ipswich and then joined Liverpool before returning in 1982.
11 Dave Watson (his manager was Norwich City's Ken Brown).

1 AiyegbeniYakubu, for £11.25 million from Middlesbrough.
2 Vinny Samways.
3 Adrian Heath moved to RCD Espanyol, and had previously cost £750,000 from Stoke in 1982.
4 Alex Nyarko.
5 Gary Megson, from Plymouth.
6 Mark Ward.
7 Derek Mountfield and Andy Gray (Aston Villa).
8 Ken McNaught.
9 Alan Stubbs, from Sunderland.
10 Mickey Walsh.
11 David Burrows (the other one, by the way, is goalkeeper Paul Jones in 2003/04).

# We love the 1970s

1  1971.

2  Asa Hartford.

3  Gordon Lee – luckily the Everton boss never drove the team bus!

4  Hillsborough.

5  Southampton. We scored only 37 league goals that season, with 8 in one game!

6  Chelsea. Bob was the first player for six years to reach the landmark in the top-flight.

7  It was the first Sunday match played by the Toffees, due to the restrictions in power supply during the economic crisis at the time. We and Liverpool therefore could not play at home at the same time during the FA Cup.

8  Mick Lyons.

9  Mark Higgins – the centre half captained us in the early 1980s before injury ended his Everton career.

10  AC Milan.

11  Joe Royle.

# Our Greatest Season Ever

1  All of them. It was the second (and final) time that this had been achieved in a top-flight of twenty-two clubs. Curiously, we were also the first team to do it, in the 1969/70 title-winning season.

2  Liverpool's Bruce Grobelaar's own goal decided the Charity Shield at Wembley.

3  We wore our away kit at Goodison, in order to avoid a colour clash.

4  Graeme Sharp.

5  Paul Wilkinson. The striker had also scored the only goal for Grimsby in a League Cup tie in November 1984 before moving to Everton.

6  The twenty-man brawl at QPR's Loftus Road saw Everton's Pat van den Hauwe dismissed.

7  West Ham United.

8  Kevin Richardson, he scored the winner at Chelsea, and both goals in a 2–1 win at Southampton and in a 1–1 draw at Aston Villa.

9  Andy Gray, after Leicester had just equalised with a goal that appeared to be offside.

10  Neville Southall.

11  Ipswich Town – a work of genius from the Irishman.

# Overseas Blues

1 Andrei Kanchelskis in a 5–2 win at Sheffield Wednesday.
2 Brazil.
3 Sweden. Niclas Alexandersson, Jesper Blomqvist and Tobias Linderoth all played in the home game against Switzerland.
4 Robert Warzycha. When scoring at Manchester United he became the first Polish player to net in the Premier League.
5 Steven Pienaar, for host nation South Africa against Mexico.
6 Thomas Gravesen, at Blackburn in November 2003.
7 Segundo Castillo.
8 Perugia.
9 Lars Jacobsen. The Dane played 5 Premier League games before his last appearance against Chelsea in the 2009 final.
10 Mikel Arteta.
11 Aston Villa and Sunderland.

1 1961 – Moores sacked Carey in the back of a London taxi.
2 Burnden Park, Bolton.
3 Roy Vernon.
4 Fred Pickering, having signed in the March.
5 Howard Kendall.
6 Alan Ball.
7 Leicester City – 1 of only 3 games in which Peter Shilton conceded 7 goals in his thirty-year career.
8 Dunfermline Athletic.
9 Blackpool.
10 Mike Trebilcock, hero of Wembley 1966.
11 *The Golden Vision*, the famous BBC *Play for Today*, based around the worship of Everton legend Alex Young, from whose nickname it was derived.

# The 1980s and 1990s Finals

1 Stuart McCall.
2 Kevin Ratcliffe, Trevor Steven and Graeme Sharp.
3 Graham Stuart.
4 Adrian Heath, who came on for Gary Stevens.
5 John Barnes, the England winger doing so for Watford in 1984 and Liverpool five years later.
6 John Bailey, who also wore a large Everton top-hat.
7 Paul Bracewell, the midfielder had started his Everton career in the Charity Shield in 1984.
8 Mark Hughes.
9 Bobby Mimms.
10 Kevin Richardson. The midfielder injured his wrist in the League Cup semi-final and it was ruled his plaster cast needed to be covered by a long-sleeved shirt. The others wore specially designed short-sleeve shirts.
11 Steve Bruce, who had played for Gillingham in the fourth round in 1984. The defender is the only player to appear against Everton in two winning FA Cup runs.

1 Leighton Baines, the full-back doing so when netting against Cheltenham Town.
2 The 1994/95 campaign.
3 Joleon Lescott.
4 Andy Gray.
5 Duncan McKenzie.
6 The floodlights failed, stopping the game for some 14 minutes.
7 Brazil and Japan in the Umbro Cup.
8 Matt Jackson, against Bristol City and Spurs in the semi-final.
9 Alan and Michael Ball.
10 Marco Materazzi.
11 Leon Osman.

# Penalty Prizes

1 Trevor Steven and David Unsworth.
2 West Brom.
3 Mikel Arteta and a debuting Jô.
4 Andy Johnson.
5 Aiyegbeni Yakubu, for Middlesbrough in 2006 and twice for the Toffees.
6 James Milner.
7 Roy Vernon.
8 Alan Ball, who ten years earlier had also missed for Arsenal against Everton.
9 Johnny Morrissey.
10 Anders Limpar.
11 Ibrahim Bakayoko.

# The Moyes Years

1  Chelsea.
2  Steve Watson.
3  Steven Pienaar. Curiously, Victor Anichebe scored in both games.
4  The 2008/09 season. This only happened before in 1914/15, 1957/58 and 1992/93.
5  Sunderland.
6  Louis Saha.
7  Hull City – the other game was a 3–2 defeat.
8  Newcastle United.
9  James Beattie.
10  Wrexham.
11  Manchester City.

# The League Cup

1  Adrian Heath. He scored at Arsenal in 1988, having netted against Southampton at Highbury four years before.
2  Neville Southall.
3  Johnny Heitinga.
4  Kevin Mirallas.
5  Chelsea, in 2007/08.
6  Paul Rideout.
7  Both sides missed penalties – Leighton Baines for Everton and Nicolas Anelka for Chelsea.
8  George Wood.
9  Coventry City, the Toffees won 2–1.
10  James McFadden.
11  John Gidman.

# A Mixed Bag of Toffees

1  Leon Osman – only Ray Wilson and Peter Reid were older when with the club.
2  Jimmy Gabriel.
3  Derek Mountfield – the Toffees won both games.
4  Kevin Campbell in 1998/99.
5  David Weir, who left to join Glasgow Rangers.
6  Purple, in honour of the Liverpool Unites Charity.
7  Goalkeeper Paul Gerrard.
8  Blackburn Rovers.
9  Australia, having been there in 1964 and 1987.
10  Colin Harvey.
11  Cliff Britton, between 1948 and 1956.

# Academy for Boys

1  Jack Rodwell, who was aged 17 years 341 days.
2  West Brom.
3  Jose Baxter.
4  Francis Jeffers, who was on loan from Arsenal, having played for Everton from 1997–2001.
5  Wayne Rooney.
6  James Vaughan.
7  Danny Cadamarteri, who was 18 years 6 days.
8  Michael Ball.
9  Richard Dunne, who scored 2 goals for the Republic of Ireland.
10  Phil Jevons.
11  Peter Clarke.

1 Newcastle United.
2 Manchester United.
3 Manchester City.
4 Duncan McKenzie.
5 Andy King.
6 Brian Kidd. He also became the first player to be sent off twice in the same FA Cup competition, having previously been dismissed against Wigan in the fourth round.
7 Peter Eastoe.
8 Hafnia (some cynics joked: 'Everton hafnia won anything for a long time').
9 Kevin Ratcliffe.
10 Wimbledon.
11 Martin Dobson.

# Premier League Toffees

1   David Unsworth.
2   Gareth Farrelly scored and Nick Barmby missed from the spot.
3   Swindon Town.
4   West Ham United.
5   Blackburn Rovers – debutant Iain Turner was sent off and replaced by fellow new boy John Ruddy.
6   The Norwegian Thomas Myhre, from 1997–2001.
7   Andrei Kanchelskis.
8   Earl Barrett.
9   Steven Piennar, with Nikica Jelavic scoring the 1,001st just seconds later.
10  QPR – Andy Sinton, Les Ferdinand and Bradley Allen.
11  Tim Howard – against Bolton!

# The Number Nines

1  Blackpool.
2  Jim Pearson.
3  SK Brann Bergen.
4  Sheffield Wednesday in 1986.
5  Andy Johnson.
6  Swansea City.
7  Joe Royle in a 2–0 victory, after which the Everton Board
   announced that Gordon Lee's position was under review.
8  Imre Varadi. The speedy early 1980s striker was known
   for his erratic finishing.
9  Roy Vernon, who was also known for smoking in the showers.
10 Manchester City.
11 Spurs.

1   Tim Cahill, for Australia against Japan – he scored their second just 5 minutes later.
2   Tim Howard in 2010.
3   Graeme Sharp, for Scotland. He made 1 appearance against Uruguay.
4   Gary Lineker, with 6 in the 1986 final stages.
5   Anders Limpar, for Sweden.
6   Tommy Wright, who replaced Keith Newton.
7   Lee Carsley.
8   AiyegbeniYakubu, for Nigeria against South Korea.
9   Johnny Heitinga in 2010.
10  Marco Materazzi, who netted for Italy in 2006 against France.
11  Stuart McCall in 1990 against Sweden.

1 Coventry City, with Wayne Clarke scoring the only goal for Everton.
2 Ray Atteveld, from Haarlem.
3 Fewest goals conceded in a league campaign – just 27 in 40 matches.
4 Sheffield Wednesday – once in the League and four times in the FA Cup.
5 Mike Newell.
6 Pat Nevin, from Chelsea.
7 Norman Whiteside. The Northern Ireland international retired from the game a year later through injury.
8 Wayne Clarke. His goal meant that Liverpool equalled Leeds' record run of 29 unbeaten games from 1973/74. In the Leeds' side was Wayne's brother, Allan.
9 Kevin Ratcliffe, whose only 2 goals for the club came away from home.
10 Vinnie Jones – who else – for Wimbledon.
11 Newcastle United.

## Round 22

# The Magic of the FA Cup

1 Phil Jagielka.
2 Joleon Lescott, in the fourth round in 2008/09.
3 Luton Town.
4 Daniel Amokachi, who famously came on the pitch while Paul Rideout was receiving treatment in the semi-final against Spurs and then scored twice.
5 Martin Hodge, for Everton in 1980 and Sheffield Wednesday in 1986.
6 Louis Saha, who scored against Middlesbrough and Chelsea.
7 Tamworth, with the Toffees winning 2–0 in the third round.
8 Middlesbrough.
9 Graeme Sharp.
10 Imre Varadi. He mistakenly ran towards a group of Liverpool fans.
11 Roger Kenyon.

1  Edwin van der Sar.
2  Royston Drenthe – the fastest since Peter Scott, after just 37 seconds against Crystal Palace in 1972.
3  Pat van den Hauwe.
4  Aiyegbeni Yakubu.
5  Howard Kendall.
6  Olivier Dacourt.
7  Kevin Campbell.
8  Chris Sutton.
9  John Ebbrell.
10  Just 25 seconds.
11  Johnny Morrissey.

# Round 24  Toffees in Europe

1. Tony Hibbert.
2. Graeme Sharp.
3. Trevor Steven.
4. Finn Harps – 5–0 in both legs.
5. Ibrahim Bakayoko.
6. Alan Ball.
7. Feyenoord.
8. Sylvain Distin.
9. John Hurst.
10. Jack Rodwell.
11. Lee Carsley.

# Celtic Toffees

1  Seamus Coleman.
2  Simon Davies, who moved to Fulham.
3  Terry Phelan.
4  Mark Pembridge.
5  Kevin Kilbane, who moved to Wigan Athletic.
6  Barry Horne against Sheffield Wednesday in 1992.
7  Michael Walsh (1978–79) and (1981–83).
8  Gary Speed against Southampton in 1996.
9  Eamonn O'Keefe, who was barred having played semi-professional football for England.
10  Mickey Thomas. He left the club after refusing to play in a reserve-team game.
11  Kevin Sheedy, who was born in Builth Wells but qualified as his father was Irish.

# The Championship Years

1 Queens Park Rangers.
2 Joe Royle.
3 Gordon West.
4 Kevin Langley.
5 Tottenham Hotspur.
6 Wayne Clarke.
7 Five – Derby County, West Brom, Liverpool, Leeds and Southampton.
8 Tony Kay.
9 Kevin Ratcliffe.
10 Tommy Lawton.
11 Johnny Morrissey.

1  Tim Cahill.
2  Neville Southall.
3  David Unsworth at Goodison in 2000/01 and 2002/03.
4  Mikel Arteta.
5  Joe Royle, who won 2 and drew 3 of his 5 games in charge.
6  Leon Osman in 2012.
7  Andy King.
8  Garry Stanley. The only previous dismissal had been Alf
   Milward of Everton in 1896.
9  Paul and Steven Gerrard.
10 Adrian Heath.
11 Dave Watson, whose brother Alex was an unused
   substitute for Liverpool.

# The Toffees and Manchester

1  Marouane Fellaini.
2  Peter Beardsley .
3  Gary Neville, for striking the ball in the direction of spectators.
4  Dan Gosling and Jack Rodwell.
5  Richard Wright, although he did not play a first–team game.
6  Leighton Baines.
7  Andy Hinchcliffe.
8  Four. Both goalkeepers were substituted for the first time in history. Andy Dibble replaced Martyn Margetson in the City goal with Jason Kearton replacing Neville Southall for the Toffees.
9  Michael Ball.
10  Mick Lyons.
11  Mark Higgins, the defender made a comeback after originally retiring through injury the previous season.

# Who Am I?

1   Marcus Bent. He netted 6 league goals for Everton in the 2004/05 season.

2   Joe Parkinson. A highly competitive midfielder with great skill whose career was cruelly ended early due to injury.

3   Niclas Alexandersson. The Swede who joined in 2000 from Sheffield Wednesday, scored for his country against England at the 2002 World Cup.

4   Alessandro Pistone. The Italian defender signed from Newcastle, who was released by the club in 2005 but joined again shortly after, only to be injured at Bolton.

5   Alex Young. The 'Golden Vision' who scored 89 goals in 275 games.

6   Trevor Steven. The midfielder who was born in Berwick-on-Tweed and won two championships at Everton, and further titles at Rangers and Marseilles.

7   Martin Keown. He scored no goals in 126 Everton games but scored for England in 1992.

8   Martin Dobson. He signed from Burnley for £300,000 in 1974 and returned there five years later.

9   Dai Davies. Toffees' goalkeeper during the 1970s.

10  Louis Saha. Played for Newcastle in 1999 and joined Everton from Manchester United in 2008. He later played for Sunderland.

11  Graham Stuart. Nicknamed 'Diamond', he scored twice against Wimbledon on the vital final day of the 1993/94 season.

1 Hearts.
2 Don Hutchison – both in 1999, on his debut in Germany and then in the play-off for Euro 2000 at Wembley.
3 Dumbarton.
4 Pat Nevin.
5 Ian Wilson.
6 John Connolly.
7 Scot Gemmill.
8 James McFadden, the pick being that strike in Paris against France.
9 John Collins.
10 Bradford City.
11 John McLaughlin. Once described, perhaps unfairly, in one newspaper thus: 'McLaughlin is only 23, but because of his bald head he looks like a man who is past it.'

1  Vinny Samways, in the 1995 Charity Shield against Blackburn Rovers.
2  Joleon Lescott.
3  Aiyegbeni Yakubu.
4  Kenny Sansom, who made 7 appearances for Everton. Curiously, his only other goal on the ground was into his own net when playing for Arsenal in a 1981 FA Cup tie.
5  Andy Gray, with a last-minute equaliser.
6  Tim Cahill.
7  Peter Reid.
8  Mikael Madar.
9  Kevin Richardson.
10  Peter Beardsley.
11  Martin Dobson.

1   Paul Gerrard, who had just signed from Oldham in a
    £1 million deal.
2   Andy Rankin.
3   Stefan Wessels.
4   Bobby Mimms (Everton in 1986/87 and Blackburn Rovers
    in 1994/95).
5   Jason Kearton.
6   Jim McDonagh.
7   Huddersfield Town.
8   Stoke City.
9   Espen Baardsen.
10  Richard Wright.
11  Jim Arnold.

1 Ted Sagar.
2 Richard Gough.
3 Goalkeeper Carlo Nash.
4 David Weir.
5 Sylvain Distin, against Leeds United.
6 Howard Kendall, who was making his last appearance as a player-manager.
7 Sandy Brown.
8 Alan Stubbs.
9 Louis Saha, in his 4 goals against Blackpool in February 2011.
10 Dave Watson (1986–2000).
11 David Ginola.

1. Liverpool, with a 1–0 victory in 1991 after an epic 4–4 draw in the first replay. It was also the last second replay in FA Cup history, as penalties were introduced in the following season after 2 games.

2. Wright – Tommy (1960s) Bernie (1970s) Billy (1980s) Mark (one game in 1990) and Richard (2000s).

3. Paul Bracewell – Sunderland was the club involved.

4. Steven Pienaar, from Borussia Dortmund on loan in 2007, a permanent deal a year later, a loan from Spurs in January 2012 and another permanent deal in the summer.

5. Duncan Ferguson, against Bolton on Boxing Day 1997.

6. Lee Carsley, on the opening day against Arsenal and in the final game against Bolton.

7. Billy Kenny, senior and junior.

8. Manchester City in January 2012.

9. American Tim Howard – over 70 at the end of the 2012/13 season.

10. Tony Cottee.

11. Victor Anichebe, for Nigeria.

1  Daniel Amokachi.
2  Alan Shearer and Les Ferdinand.
3  Elland Road.
4  Tony Hibbert – 2000/01 to 2009/10.
5  Leon Osman – 2003/04 to 2012/13.
6  Joseph Yobo.
7  Newcastle United.
8  Arsenal in May 2005.
9  Nikica Jelavic.
10  Duncan Ferguson.
11  Manchester City.

# What's the Link?

1 They all scored their first Everton goals against Liverpool.
2 They were all signed from Derby County.
3 All missed the first penalty in shoot-outs where Everton later emerged victorious.
4 All teams that Gary Lineker scored hat-tricks against for Everton.
5 They knocked Everton out of the FA Cup in matches played at Goodison.
6 Players who scored the winning goals in Anfield derby matches.
7 They all scored on their Everton debuts on the opening day of the season.
8 The first league games in charge as manager for Howard Kendall, Colin Harvey and Mike Walker.
9 Were all transferred to Manchester City.
10 They all unfortunately scored own goals in derby games.
11 Teams that have played against Everton at Wembley – Manchester City (1933 FA Cup final), Nottingham Forest (1989 Simod Cup final) and Crystal Palace (1991 ZDS Cup final).

1 Sunderland.
2 Aston Villa.
3 Watford.
4 Arsenal.
5 Sheffield Wednesday. It was once the most-played fixture in FA Cup history, before being overtaken by the Merseyside derby.
6 Carlisle, who won 3–2 at Goodison and 3–0 at Brunton Park.
7 Manchester United in the 1964/65 Fairs Cup – United won 3–2 on aggregate.
8 Arsenal.
9 AZ67 Alkmaar.
10 QPR.
11 Fulham.

## Round 38

# The HK File

1  Preston North End.
2  West Ham United in September 1967.
3  Sheffield United.
4  Adrian Heath.
5  1972.
6  Manchester United, in the 1985 Charity Shield.
7  Mike Lyons.
8  A total of 4 times – 1 as a player in 1968, and 3 as a manager in the 1980s.
9  Thomas Myhre.
10  1968.
11  Bryan Ferry. They both attended the Washington Grammar-Technical School in County Durham.

# More Derby Madnees

1  Gary Lineker and Andrei Kanchelskis.
2  Maine Road – the 1984 League Cup final replay.
3  Ibrahim Bakayoko.
4  Sylvain Distin.
5  Wayne Rooney.
6  David Johnson. He scored the winning goals in the two team's most recent derby victories at the time: Everton's 1–0 victory in November 1971 and Liverpool's 1–0 win in April 1978.
7  1967.
8  Alan Harper.
9  Dave Watson, at Goodison in April 1997.
10  Kevin Ratcliffe.
11  Graeme Sharp, in the 4–4 draw in February 1991.

1  Royston Drenthe.
2  Dan Gosling, in the famous 1–0 FA Cup win over Liverpool.
3  Aston Villa.
4  Leighton Baines.
5  Jermaine Beckford.
6  Birmingham City – Lee Carsley and James Vaughan were the scorers.
7  Diniyar Bilyaletdinov.
8  Manchester City.
9  Mikel Arteta.
10  Charlton Athletic.
11  Leon Osman.

Lightning Source UK Ltd.
Milton Keynes UK
UKOW06f1819271217
315163UK00010B/278/P